TRAMPOLINE

GYMNASTICS GOALBOOK

© Dream Co Publishing 2020. ISBN 978-0-9951317-4-3

Sports club bulk orders: orders@dreamcomedia.nz

Image credit: Valeriya Novozhonova/Alex Emanuel Koch/Shutterstock.com

Contents:

Info	page 1
Encouraging quotes	page 2
Yearly Training Goals	page 4
Training Goals	page 8
Competition Goals	page 64

Gymnastics Info:

Name: _____

Age: _____

Level: _____

Club: _____

Coach/es: _____

Favourite skill/s: _____

_____

Favourite trampoline event/s: _____

_____

Favourite Olympic gymnast: _____

_____

Favourite training outfit: _____

Inspirational words or quotes:

Inspirational words or quotes:

My Yearly Training Goals:

Date: _____

_____
_____
_____
_____
_____
_____
_____
_____
_____
_____
_____
_____
_____
_____
_____

◇ *You can do it!* ◇

My Yearly Training Outcomes:

Date: _____

_____
_____
_____
_____
_____
_____
_____
_____
_____
_____
_____
_____
_____
_____

◇ *Go for gold!* ◇

My Yearly Training Goals:

Date: _____

_____
_____
_____
_____
_____
_____
_____
_____
_____
_____
_____
_____
_____
_____
_____
_____
_____
_____
_____
_____

◇ Dreams are possible. ◇

My Yearly Training Outcomes:

Date: _____

_____

_____

_____

_____

_____

_____

_____

_____

_____

_____

_____

_____

_____

_____

_____

◇ Flipping out is fun! ◇

My Training Goals:

Date: _____

_____
_____
_____
_____
_____
_____
_____
_____
_____
_____
_____
_____
_____
_____
_____

◇ *Don't give up!* ◇

My Training Outcomes:

Date: _____

_____
_____
_____
_____
_____
_____
_____
_____
_____
_____
_____
_____
_____
_____
_____
_____
_____
_____

◇ *Train like a champion.* ◇

My Training Goals:

Date: _____

_____
_____
_____
_____
_____
_____
_____
_____
_____
_____
_____
_____
_____
_____
_____
_____

◇　*Aim high!*　◇

My Training Outcomes:

Date: _____

_____
_____
_____
_____
_____
_____
_____
_____
_____
_____
_____
_____
_____
_____
_____
_____

◇ You're a star! ◇

My Training Goals:

Date: _____

_____
_____
_____
_____
_____
_____
_____
_____
_____
_____
_____
_____
_____
_____
_____
_____
_____
_____

◇ *If you don't try — you won't know what you're actually capable of.* ◇

My Training Outcomes:

Date: _____

_____
_____
_____
_____
_____
_____
_____
_____
_____
_____
_____
_____
_____
_____
_____
_____

◇ *You got this!* ◇

My Training Goals:

Date: _____

_____
_____
_____
_____
_____
_____
_____
_____
_____
_____
_____
_____
_____
_____
_____
_____

◇ *You're amazing.* ◇

My Training Outcomes:

Date: _____

_____
_____
_____
_____
_____
_____
_____
_____
_____
_____
_____
_____
_____
_____
_____
_____

◇ Believe – achieve. ◇

My Training Goals:

Date: _____

_____
_____
_____
_____
_____
_____
_____
_____
_____
_____
_____
_____
_____
_____
_____
_____

◇ ...it's a gymnast thing. ◇

My Training Outcomes:

Date: _____

_____
_____
_____
_____
_____
_____
_____
_____
_____
_____
_____
_____
_____
_____
_____

◇ Be flexible, be strong. And smile! ◇

My Training Goals:

Date: _____

_____
_____
_____
_____
_____
_____
_____
_____
_____
_____
_____
_____
_____
_____
_____
_____
_____
_____

◇ *You can do it!* ◇

My Training Outcomes:

Date: _____

_____
_____
_____
_____
_____
_____
_____
_____
_____
_____
_____
_____
_____
_____
_____

◇ *Go for gold!* ◇

My Training Goals:

Date: _____

_____
_____
_____
_____
_____
_____
_____
_____
_____
_____
_____
_____
_____
_____
_____
_____

◇ Dreams are possible. ◇

My Training Outcomes:

Date: _____

_____
_____
_____
_____
_____
_____
_____
_____
_____
_____
_____
_____
_____
_____
_____

◇ Flipping out is fun! ◇

My Training Goals:

Date: _____

_____
_____
_____
_____
_____
_____
_____
_____
_____
_____
_____
_____
_____
_____
_____

◇ Don't give up! ◇

My Training Outcomes:

Date: _____

_____
_____
_____
_____
_____
_____
_____
_____
_____
_____
_____
_____
_____
_____
_____
_____

◇ *Train like a champion.* ◇

My Training Goals:

Date: _____

_____
_____
_____
_____
_____
_____
_____
_____
_____
_____
_____
_____
_____
_____
_____
_____

◇ **Aim high!** ◇

My Training Outcomes:

Date: _____

_____
_____
_____
_____
_____
_____
_____
_____
_____
_____
_____
_____
_____
_____
_____
_____

◇ You're a star! ◇

My Training Goals:

Date: _____

_____
_____
_____
_____
_____
_____
_____
_____
_____
_____
_____
_____
_____
_____
_____

◇ Trampolining counts as flying. ◇

My Training Outcomes:

Date: _____

_____
_____
_____
_____
_____
_____
_____
_____
_____
_____
_____
_____
_____
_____
_____

◇ *I love gymnastics!* ◇

My Training Goals:

Date: _____

_____
_____
_____
_____
_____
_____
_____
_____
_____
_____
_____
_____
_____
_____
_____

◇ *If you don't try — you won't know what you're actually capable of.* ◇

My Training Outcomes:

Date: _____

_____
_____
_____
_____
_____
_____
_____
_____
_____
_____
_____
_____
_____
_____
_____
_____

◇ *You got this!* ◇

My Training Goals:

Date: _____

_____
_____
_____
_____
_____
_____
_____
_____
_____
_____
_____
_____
_____
_____
_____

◇ Trampolining is the best! ◇

My Training Outcomes:

Date: _____

_____
_____
_____
_____
_____
_____
_____
_____
_____
_____
_____
_____
_____
_____

◇ **Don't forget to have fun.** ◇

My Training Goals:

Date: _____

_____
_____
_____
_____
_____
_____
_____
_____
_____
_____
_____
_____
_____
_____
_____

◇ *Run towards a challenge, not away from it.* ◇

My Training Outcomes:

Date: _____

_____
_____
_____
_____
_____
_____
_____
_____
_____
_____
_____
_____
_____
_____
_____
_____

◇ *Fly like an eagle.* ◇

My Training Goals:

Date: _____

_____
_____
_____
_____
_____
_____
_____
_____
_____
_____
_____
_____
_____
_____
_____

◇ You're amazing. ◇

My Training Outcomes:

Date: _____

_____
_____
_____
_____
_____
_____
_____
_____
_____
_____
_____
_____
_____
_____
_____

◇ Believe — achieve. ◇

My Training Goals:

Date: _____

_____
_____
_____
_____
_____
_____
_____
_____
_____
_____
_____
_____
_____
_____
_____

◇ ...it's a gymnast thing. ◇

My Training Outcomes:

Date: _____

_____
_____
_____
_____
_____
_____
_____
_____
_____
_____
_____
_____
_____
_____
_____

◇ Be flexible, be strong. And smile! ◇

My Training Goals:

Date: _____

_____
_____
_____
_____
_____
_____
_____
_____
_____
_____
_____
_____
_____
_____
_____

◇ *You can do it!* ◇

My Training Outcomes:

Date: _____

_____
_____
_____
_____
_____
_____
_____
_____
_____
_____
_____
_____
_____
_____
_____
_____

◇ *Go for gold!* ◇

My Training Goals:

Date: _____

_____
_____
_____
_____
_____
_____
_____
_____
_____
_____
_____
_____
_____
_____
_____

◇ Dreams are possible. ◇

My Training Outcomes:

Date: _____

_____
_____
_____
_____
_____
_____
_____
_____
_____
_____
_____
_____
_____
_____
_____

◇ Flipping out is fun! ◇

My Training Goals:

Date: _____

_____
_____
_____
_____
_____
_____
_____
_____
_____
_____
_____
_____
_____
_____

◇ *Don't give up!* ◇

My Training Outcomes:

Date: _____

_____
_____
_____
_____
_____
_____
_____
_____
_____
_____
_____
_____
_____
_____
_____

◇ *Train like a champion.* ◇

My Training Goals:

Date: _____

_____
_____
_____
_____
_____
_____
_____
_____
_____
_____
_____
_____
_____
_____
_____
_____
_____

◇ **Aim high!** ◇

My Training Outcomes:

Date: _____

_____
_____
_____
_____
_____
_____
_____
_____
_____
_____
_____
_____
_____
_____
_____
_____

◇ You're a star! ◇

My Training Goals:

Date: _____

◇ *Trampolining counts as flying.* ◇

My Training Outcomes:

Date: _____

◇ *I love trampolining!* ◇

My Training Goals:

Date: _____

_____
_____
_____
_____
_____
_____
_____
_____
_____
_____
_____
_____
_____
_____
_____
_____

◇ *If you don't try — you won't know what you're actually capable of.* ◇

My Training Outcomes:

Date: _____

_____
_____
_____
_____
_____
_____
_____
_____
_____
_____
_____
_____
_____
_____
_____

◇ You got this! ◇

My Training Goals:

Date: _____

_____
_____
_____
_____
_____
_____
_____
_____
_____
_____
_____
_____
_____
_____
_____
_____

◇ *Trampolining is the best!* ◇

My Training Outcomes:

Date: _____

◇ Don't forget to have fun. ◇

My Training Goals:

Date: _____

_____
_____
_____
_____
_____
_____
_____
_____
_____
_____
_____
_____
_____
_____
_____

◇ Run towards a challenge, not away from it. ◇

My Training Outcomes:

Date: _____

◇ Trampolining counts as flying. ◇

My Training Goals:

Date: _____

_____
_____
_____
_____
_____
_____
_____
_____
_____
_____
_____
_____
_____
_____
_____
_____

◇ You're amazing. ◇

My Training Outcomes:

Date: _____

_____
_____
_____
_____
_____
_____
_____
_____
_____
_____
_____
_____
_____
_____
_____

◇ Believe — achieve. ◇

My Training Goals:

Date: _____

_____
_____
_____
_____
_____
_____
_____
_____
_____
_____
_____
_____
_____
_____
_____
_____

◇ ...it's a gymnast thing. ◇

My Training Outcomes:

Date: _____

_____
_____
_____
_____
_____
_____
_____
_____
_____
_____
_____
_____
_____
_____
_____

◇ Be flexible, be strong. And smile! ◇

My Training Goals:

Date: _____

_____
_____
_____
_____
_____
_____
_____
_____
_____
_____
_____
_____
_____
_____
_____

◇ *You can do it!* ◇

My Training Outcomes:

Date: _____

_____
_____
_____
_____
_____
_____
_____
_____
_____
_____
_____
_____
_____
_____
_____

◇ *Go for gold!* ◇

My Training Goals:

Date: _____

_____
_____
_____
_____
_____
_____
_____
_____
_____
_____
_____
_____
_____
_____
_____
_____
_____

◇ Dreams are possible. ◇

My Training Outcomes:

Date: _____

_____
_____
_____
_____
_____
_____
_____
_____
_____
_____
_____
_____
_____
_____
_____
_____

◇ *Flipping out is fun!* ◇

My Training Goals:

Date: _____

_____
_____
_____
_____
_____
_____
_____
_____
_____
_____
_____
_____
_____
_____
_____

◇ *Don't give up!* ◇

My Training Outcomes:

Date: _____

_____
_____
_____
_____
_____
_____
_____
_____
_____
_____
_____
_____
_____
_____
_____
_____
_____

◇ *Train like a champion.* ◇

My Competition Goals:

Date: _____

Competition name: _____

_____
_____
_____
_____
_____
_____
_____
_____
_____
_____
_____
_____

COMMENTS: _____
_____

◇ *Trampolining counts as flying.* ◇

My Competition Achievements:

Date: _____

Competition name: _____

_____
_____
_____
_____
_____
_____
_____
_____
_____
_____
_____
_____
_____

SCORES: _____
_____

◇ *I love gymnastics!* ◇

My Competition Goals:

Date: _____

Competition name: _____

_____
_____
_____
_____
_____
_____
_____
_____
_____
_____
_____
_____

COMMENTS: _____
_____

◇ *If you don't try — you won't know what you're actually capable of.* ◇

My Competition Achievements:

Date: _____

Competition name: _____

_____
_____
_____
_____
_____
_____
_____
_____
_____
_____
_____
_____
_____

SCORES: _____
_____

◇ *You got this!* ◇

My Competition Goals:

Date: _____

Competition name: _____

_____
_____
_____
_____
_____
_____
_____
_____
_____
_____
_____
_____
_____

COMMENTS: _____
_____

◇ Trampolining is the best! ◇

My Competition Achievements:

Date: _____

Competition name: _____

_____
_____
_____
_____
_____
_____
_____
_____
_____
_____
_____
_____
_____

SCORES: _____
_____

◇ *Don't forget to have fun.* ◇

My Competition Goals:

Date: _____

Competition name: _____

_____
_____
_____
_____
_____
_____
_____
_____
_____
_____
_____
_____

COMMENTS: _____
_____

◇ *Run towards a challenge, not away from it.* ◇

My Competition Achievements:

Date: _____

Competition name: _____

_____

_____

_____

_____

_____

_____

_____

_____

_____

_____

_____

SCORES: _____

_____

◇ *Fly like an eagle.* ◇

My Competition Goals:

Date: _____

Competition name: _____

_____
_____
_____
_____
_____
_____
_____
_____
_____
_____
_____
_____

COMMENTS: _____
_____

◇ *You're amazing.* ◇

My Competition Achievements:

Date: _____

Competition name: _____

_____
_____
_____
_____
_____
_____
_____
_____
_____
_____
_____
_____
_____

SCORES: _____
_____

◇ Believe — achieve. ◇

My Competition Goals:

Date: _____

Competition name: _____

_____

_____

_____

_____

_____

_____

_____

_____

_____

_____

_____

_____

COMMENTS: _____

_____

◇ ...it's a gymnast thing. ◇

My Competition Achievements:

Date: _____

Competition name: _____

_____

_____

_____

_____

_____

_____

_____

_____

_____

_____

_____

_____

_____

SCORES: _____

_____

◇ Be flexible, be strong. And smile! ◇

My Competition Goals:

Date: _____

Competition name: _____

_____
_____
_____
_____
_____
_____
_____
_____
_____
_____
_____
_____

COMMENTS: _____
_____

◇ *You can do it!* ◇

My Competition Achievements:

Date: _____

Competition name: _____

_____

_____

_____

_____

_____

_____

_____

_____

_____

_____

_____

_____

SCORES: _____

_____

◇   *Go for gold!*   ◇

My Competition Goals:

Date: _____

Competition name: _____

_____
_____
_____
_____
_____
_____
_____
_____
_____
_____
_____
_____
_____

COMMENTS: _____
_____

◇ Dreams are possible. ◇

My Competition Achievements:

Date: _____

Competition name: _____

_____
_____
_____
_____
_____
_____
_____
_____
_____
_____
_____
_____
_____

SCORES: _____
_____

◇ *Flipping out is fun!* ◇

My Competition Goals:

Date: _____

Competition name: _____

_____
_____
_____
_____
_____
_____
_____
_____
_____
_____
_____
_____

COMMENTS: _____
_____

◇ *Don't give up!* ◇

My Competition Achievements:

Date: _____

Competition name: _____

_____

_____

_____

_____

_____

_____

_____

_____

_____

_____

_____

_____

SCORES: _____

_____

◇ *Train like a champion.* ◇

My Competition Goals:

Date: _____

Competition name: _____

_____
_____
_____
_____
_____
_____
_____
_____
_____
_____
_____
_____

COMMENTS: _____
_____

◇   *Aim high!*   ◇

My Competition Achievements:

Date: _____

Competition name: _____

_____
_____
_____
_____
_____
_____
_____
_____
_____
_____
_____
_____
_____

SCORES: _____
_____

◇ *You're a star!* ◇

My Competition Goals:

Date: _____

Competition name: _____

_____
_____
_____
_____
_____
_____
_____
_____
_____
_____
_____

COMMENTS: _____
_____

◇ *Trampolining counts as flying.* ◇

My Competition Achievements:

Date: _____

Competition name: _____

_____

_____

_____

_____

_____

_____

_____

_____

_____

_____

_____

_____

_____

SCORES: _____

_____

◇ *I love trampolining!* ◇

My Competition Goals:

Date: _____

Competition name: _____

_____

_____

_____

_____

_____

_____

_____

_____

_____

_____

_____

COMMENTS: _____

_____

◇ *If you don't try — you won't know what you're actually capable of.* ◇

My Competition Achievements:

Date: _____

Competition name: _____

_____
_____
_____
_____
_____
_____
_____
_____
_____
_____
_____
_____
_____

SCORES: _____
_____

◇ *You got this!* ◇

My Competition Goals:

Date: _____

Competition name: _____

_____
_____
_____
_____
_____
_____
_____
_____
_____
_____
_____
_____
_____

COMMENTS: _____
_____

◇   Aim high!   ◇

My Competition Achievements:

Date: _____

Competition name: _____

_____
_____
_____
_____
_____
_____
_____
_____
_____
_____
_____
_____
_____

SCORES: _____
_____

◇ *You're a star!* ◇

My Competition Goals:

Date: _____

Competition name: _____

_____
_____
_____
_____
_____
_____
_____
_____
_____
_____
_____
_____

COMMENTS: _____
_____

◇ *Trampolining counts as flying.* ◇

My Competition Achievements:

Date: _____

Competition name: _____

_____
_____
_____
_____
_____
_____
_____
_____
_____
_____
_____
_____
_____

SCORES: _____
_____

◇ *I love gymnastics!* ◇

My Competition Goals:

Date: _____

Competition name: _____

_____
_____
_____
_____
_____
_____
_____
_____
_____
_____
_____
_____

COMMENTS: _____
_____

◇ Trampolining is the best! ◇

My Competition Achievements:

Date: _____

Competition name: _____

_____
_____
_____
_____
_____
_____
_____
_____
_____
_____
_____
_____
_____

SCORES: _____
_____

◇ *Don't forget to have fun.* ◇

My Competition Goals:

Date: _____

Competition name: _____

_____
_____
_____
_____
_____
_____
_____
_____
_____
_____
_____
_____

COMMENTS: _____
_____

◇ *Run towards a challenge, not away from it.* ◇

My Competition Achievements:

Date: _____

Competition name: _____

_____
_____
_____
_____
_____
_____
_____
_____
_____
_____
_____
_____

SCORES: _____
_____

◇ *Fly like an eagle.* ◇

Extra notes

www.ingramcontent.com/pod-product-compliance
Lightning Source LLC
Chambersburg PA
CBHW070759020526
44118CB00036B/2070